In 2008, author R. E. Smith founded New Poets Society, a non-profit organization whose purpose is to encourage and inspire high school age students to read, write and enjoy poetry. Scholarships are awarded each year to those students who have exhibited outstanding promise in literary creativity. Donations to New Poets Society are fully tax deductible. Please join us in encouraging the poets and authors of the future.

Thank you ~   **New Poets Society**
13303 NE 75th Street
Redmond, WA 98052

A Sweeter Understanding

Upcoming R. E. Smith poetry

The Window Ledge

Emily !
Just Keep Writing

A Sweeter
Understanding

R. E. SMITH

R E Smith

Sofa Ink

Vancouver, Washington

A Sweeter Understanding
by R. E. Smith

10 digit ISBN: 0-9769261-2-1
13 digit ISBN: 978-0-9769261-2-2

Edited by Linda M. Meyer

Cover design by Belle Larsen
Author photos by Jennifer Lydick. Reproduced by
permission. www.longstofly.com
Daisies, Butterflies by Gail Gibson
Interior design by David Cowsert
Publishing assistance by Meredith Norwich

Printed and bound in the United States.

Sofa Ink
PO Box 65849
Vancouver, WA 98665
www.sofaink.com

10 09 08 07 06   1 2 3 4 5

For my mother and father,
who nurtured a family of writers
and then sent us out into the world—
encouraged about our potential, patient with
our craft, and confident in our purpose.

— R. E. Smith

Table of Contents

x

Preface

Poetry is the universal language of connection, emotion, desire, and regret. It connects us with the tones and colors of life, recollections of the past, and hopes for the future.

This collection of poems paints pictures with words, little vignettes of life's simplest treasures, calling forth the pain and pleasure of a life well lived.

Each poem, each word or line, comes from a quiet place in my heart. The words have become works of love, documenting daily life, the most complicated and compelling moments endured and enjoyed.

Welcome to my journey. I am complimented by the attention you've given me, and I am honored to become part of your world. Welcome to mine. If we listen well, we can each come to share *A Sweeter Understanding*.

— *R. E. Smith*

Acknowledgments

First and foremost to my publisher, David Cowsert, who believed in this book from the start—for his belief in my work, and the time and energy to bring it to you. And to the incomparable Linda M. Meyer, who has managed to edit the work without bruising my ego and yet contributed magnificent changes to the composition.

Also, to the other members of the Gray Sunshine publishing team whose dedicated efforts made this project a success. Most notably, Meredith Norwich, who enlightened and encouraged me and otherwise provided impetus throughout the project.

I'd be remiss if I did not thank my family and a multitude of friends who believed strongly enough in me to give me courage over the years to express my view of the world in verse. For all those who gave me inspiration, may I repay you with gratitude? For all who gave me encouragement, please accept my sincere thanks. For those who gave love, I humbly ask you to accept mine in return.

For the readers with whom I've connected over the years, and to all who join me now, I hope you find a moment of reflection and celebration in the poems that follow. As this happens, we will share success.

— R. E. Smith

love matured

Each year that I grow older
I see you different than before.
Once you seemed to walk along
now you glide across the floor.
Perhaps my eyes in vision blur
your smile in shadows cast
angelic understanding of
the youth we shared that's passed.
Your touch is different, too, somehow
it reaches deep within
beyond the fragile bones contained
within my wrinkled skin.

You fill my heart and lift my hopes
well above the pain
to calm fearful anxieties
growing old can bring.
And as I share the mundane task
of every daily chore
I realize the difference is
each year I love you more.
The years have older made me now
and soon I'll pass away
but not before expressing thanks
for what we've shared each day.

love's muted memory

The breath of love expires
　　　　just beyond the ear of anticipation.
A perfect union is realized
　　　　in the understanding relationship
of the ear
　　　　and the softly uttered sigh.

Though I like to think of my writing and your reading as a shared activity, it occurred to me not to interrupt your reading with tidbits from my mind. Yet in these small notes, I invite you to share more deeply with me and I with you. In this way, we are both enriched. Unlike many face-to-face encounters, this book allows us each to explore at whim—skipping, re-reading, or considering at our convenience. Thank you for sharing this journey with me.

— R. E. S.

"i wish it would rain"

Rain
pounded like fists on the rooftop.
Wind
spoke to us like voices of caution.
Elements protected us
delaying our departure to
another boring day.

So we stayed
teaching each other to play and cuddle
losing ourselves in a playground of emotions
savoring the opportunity to talk, and listen
for more important things
than the monotony of wind and rain.

Between our hopes, dreams
and tight-fitted sheets
we learned to hold words, emotions
and each other in a delicate embrace
without expectations or limitations
sharing the splendor of tenderness
guarded by elements of whispered approval.
Oh, how I wish it would rain.

life's pretentious fool

The proportionate fool in each of us
forgets
or chooses to ignore
that water runs downhill.
We wait in vain loneliness
above ourselves
for the drink of life
to quench unreasonable thirst.
Our tongues soon parch
with the bitter-tasting truth
of our own ignorance.

the journal

Without your love
I would be a journal of lost emotion
a story of romance
without character or purpose
a book without covers
knowing neither alpha nor omega
an empty page
unwrinkled
unblemished
waiting, just waiting
for you.
You are the feeling
the ink in my life
the message and meaning
of love.

just half

Half of me wants to hold you
        half of me wants to touch.
Half of me misses you most of all
        and the other half just as much.
Half of me hurts so bad I cry
        half of me only wonders why
the other half went away.

In retrospect, we leave some of ourselves at each intersecting relationship. Our associations go in directions we cannot foresee, only reflect upon.

— R. E. S.

sisters

I've watched these girls
   whirl through life
      like hurricanes or twisters.
         To other men
            they said their vows.
               It's all right—
                  they are my sisters.

king me

You arouse in me a feeling of power
not because I am powerful
but I sense the capability of being so.
You inspire in me a feeling of majesty
not because of royal heritage
rather, bolstered by the majesty of our dreams.
You awaken in me the color of autumn leaves
still nights and deep water
that remains buried somewhere
in the length and depth of comfort shared
frozen in the time enjoined
for the miles we are yet to travel
together.

the right parts

You are a rib of the mountain
  as much as the grace note of song.
You are the breath of gentle wind
  that blows the whole night long.
You are the current of river
  that flows into the sea.
You are a part of the love I've known.
  Forever a part of me.

storms

May the strong hand of love
pick you up
hold you gently near
and let you know there is no storm
of earth, of sea, or mothered by the sky
as treacherous to face
as the storm of without you.

when i die

Bury me facing the sun
that I might bask in its warmth
On a hill
that I may be refreshed by wind and rain
Within the embrace of a tree
that animals may be close at hand
Around the corner from a playground
that laughter may ring in my ears
In range of church bells
that I may stay close to God
Next to my love
that we may go on sharing
With room for my family
to join me in time
Near life
that I won't stray far in death
or be forgotten.

the touch

The first touch is always the softest
also the most delicate.
It lasts longest in the archives of our souls.
This becomes the lace upon which
our relationships are sewn
and the subsequent touching helps develop
the tapestry we weave together, in time.

*I wrote the next poem during a time when I made many
conscious observations about the people around me. There is
much to learn from watching people.*

— R. E. S.

mountains, beaches, and me

Life has people
and mountains.
Some people
think they are mountains.
Of those
some harbor deep caves
others begin in the center of earth.
Many are barren
others infinitely beautiful
innocent in their wilderness.
Unfortunately
many people
who think they are mountains
are only beaches
running lengthwise along the shore
unable to go up or down.
I'm a people, too.
Unwilling to tear down other mountains
I quietly build my own.

procreation

If we drop a grain of sand
what wind do we play
in settling it to the earth?
If we agitate the water
what tide is ours
to move along the shore?
Days half torn by lives half shared
will not cause ripples
in sand or water.
Love is the only force
with answers of tomorrow.

night fog

Night fog
creeps on quiet wind-waves
slow to depart
the suffocated view.
Sound sneaks magnified
from the isolated
but familiar island
of graying mist
to hang carelessly
from the clothesline of imagination.

ambition

I hope never to become
a stone
against the wind of progress
to find myself
at the dawn of a new day
buried
in the settled dust
of someone else's dream.

preposterous worth

Don't measure my wealth
by the size of my wallet
by that yardstick I'd surely be poor.
Of riches bequeathed
the prizes most treasured
protected by thought's open door.
Friends that I've gathered
loves I have known
memories supplanted
happiness shown.
Gifts once received
from dreams often shared
of people I've met
who steadfastly cared.
Jewels of existence
of great influence and more
their air I shall breathe 'til I'm done.
They are my earth and my sky
the God of my love
and moments of life yet to come.

I wrote this while still a fire chief for the Port of Seattle. I felt quite satisfied with my life, my friends, and my family. This poem came easily to final form.

— R. E. S.

weakness

Of the most disappointing
   adventures in life
   few can be more depressing
   than when you must admit
   that the power of your ability
   is less than
   the extension of your reach.

pages

Beginnings are all there ever are
of what we ought to be
the doughnut holes of all the dreams
we take the time to see.

Pretend we must to understand
that crooked line to rest
on half-worn pages of yesterday
and tomorrow's untried test.

The end belongs in plays and books
read so leisurely
has ill effect on love or life
or all they mean to me.

So when the book curls corners up
wearing thin and showing age
let romance stay to lean upon
this actor's final stage.

still soft earth

Quiet time prepares our dreams
sharing more of life
than what it seems
to last in all I offer you
as flowers fresh
bless mornings new
like flowers fresh we'll rest above
still soft earth of lasting love.

Still earth holds water in
like love expressed
from deep within
evaporates where raindrops go
appearing soon
in clouds' soft glow
returning then to rest again
in still soft earth of what we've been.

relativity

You are related to birds that fly
and all things that grow
a part of froth in every wave
that rests upon the shore.
You are sister to a sun that shines
brother of the rain
you climb above thoughts of man
to rest in their disdain.
Your smile prepares a beacon's light
it shines through densest fog.
You mother every precious thought
you father every child.
You sleep within treasured dreams
then whisper to the wind.
You move mountains made of man
and make their will to bend.
To gently place a willing child
on pillowed clouds above
you are all things, to all mankind
the epitome of love.

wrought iron bed

I scratched the earth
filling the space between my finger and nail
to leave empty, a trail for dust to settle
never thinking to measure in time or effort
what Nature would take in replacement.

I made a mark
upon time's weathered face
to leave an umbrella of shadow for others to share
never wondering how many faces would be caressed
by the shape of my provision.

I slept for a while
in a wrought iron bed
to fill the world with my need
never realizing how much returned from what I left of myself
weeping in turn over wrought iron yesterday and you.

I dreamed of nights yet spent
with one face to draw me on
another to push me back, and they were equal
smiling in momentary bliss
while hands drew sheets in wonderment
over the truthful experience love provided
the unselfish voice of my echoing bewilderment.

serenity

Each snowflake sings a different song
walking where wind has never been.
Snow angels dance across the landscape
moving as the shadows fall.
Laughter echoes through the woods
from voices of the past
there to smile upon the scene
your face in image lasts.

The crunch of snow a spell does weave
of thoughts from deep within.
Silence broken in my mind
your laughter once again
reminding me to quicken pace
warms me as I view your face
from hearthside light, reflections of your love.

So I stumble on like bird with broken wing
drawing strength from my purpose
consoled by the cold of it all.
The sun shines around but never through the tree
so lonely is autumn's last leaf
hoping for winter's icy blast to finally set it free.

tiger tiger

Never dwell
on lost decisions.
On the decisive hell
of a new day
the tiger's paw
would sooner hunt tomorrow
than rip apart yesterday's empty dream.

I knew a long time ago that I couldn't sing well enough to get out of the shower. Even though I spent a few years in the high school band, I didn't learn to read music. When acting, I couldn't remember the lines. My two left feet kept me from being a dancer. When I drew, my stick man looked like a Charlie Brown Christmas tree. Artistically, I was lost.

My God-given talent took a long time to develop, and it took even longer to recognize that it is something enhanced by sharing. Today when I write, I hope it resonates with you like a favorite song or painting.

I admire many famous poets, yet I find the most inspiration from the largely unknown poets around me who write for the simple pleasure it brings and the sense of sharing it invites.

— *R. E. S.*

frustration

I am a kite string
slowly unraveling
aspiring to dizzying heights
waltzing to a wind-song
until stretched taut
between my resistance and desire
unable to break the hold
at either end of the string
I sway suspended
between a rough wind
and total frustration.

omega

Spread me through
thinning seas
      cool the drowning soul
      cool the burning birth anew
love out of control.

Pretend my eyes
to see beyond
      the sea beyond the shore
      where life awaits the fluid grace
of waves, on ocean's floor.

Fill me with
intensity
      of light both bright and slow
      of light adorning winter's crest
as trees, begin to grow.

Where birds take flight
of heaven's night
      settled in the morrow's treasure
      settled grotto of our youthful dreams
mirrored by this moment's pleasure.

As eyes weep truth
of time and motion
      before the pendulum strikes again
      before the tempered lover's notion.
The whispered quest, Omega sends.

friendship

If wanting
were all that was left of alone
I'd want the softness of you to reach me.
If knowing
helped ease the dusk of fear
you'd be bathed in thoughts of together.
An element of touch
would glue us, forever
cementing friendship's foundations.
Life would be easier to answer
using hope as a megaphone to express ourselves.
Others might learn that simplicity is beauty.
Being a friend is not always simple,
                              but a beautiful thing
not as selfish as some might imagine.

old sweet song

I see the smile of you
curve upon the happy face of life.
I've seen the soft sweet night of you
surrender perfumed dreams.
I've felt you touch quite past my heart
direct my gaze beyond the dark
like the edge of song that keeps repeating itself
in memory.
You are always. Always.

accomplishment

Don't let a strong wind of uncertainty
spoil the fragile petals of a
growing confidence.
Accomplish all you will by
leaning into the wind
to shelter the relationship
between the flower
and the fragrance of its own bouquet.

lovers

In darkened corners
of once-deserted rooms
our hearts tremble
in crescendo
as our music echoes
from an otherwise deepening silence
until all that is left
is the heavy breathing
of the romance we share.
My tongue speaks the language
your lips understand.
All that is heard is the softly uttered sigh
of loving you, and the frantic
thump, thump, thumping of my heart.

stones

Fading line of gray, distant stone
absorbed and extended
by dispassionate clouds
serve darkness lurking
beyond shadow's quieting fall
engage the retiring sunset
in the seriousness of night
where dreams are born
to the random world
of time unending.

first

Only one is first
in what is done
though many try to be.
I am first
in what I think
and everything I see.
Though not the first
to witness love
to testify it's real
is everything
you say or do
and all you make me feel.

fragmentation

I'm amazed at how fragile I've become
since knowing you.
Your hands are like dreams
wandering over my body.
My dreams are like hands
trying to hold you close.
In between the dreams
we purchase a thousand realities
always paying in full for the emotions shared.
Something hidden in the secrets
of each payment made
building memories from the treasure spent.

What cost imposed on chasing dreams
often confused by fading mists of hope?
Am I alone aware of
inevitable, encroaching loneliness
standing blinded by a fog of indecision?
Am I hanging on to what might have been
holding back tears of dissolution
waiting for division of our lives
to condense choices for us?
What was life before we met?

What would it be without you?
What plague has put upon my soul
that cannot be treated by thought
or cured by promise?
Without the skin of dreams
to hold relationships firm
we would break and crumble
in pieces on the floor.
How are we infected by this malady called love?
Aren't we even more fragile without it?

Life, like a circle, goes on.

— *R. E. S.*

recollections

How sweet
the gentle thought
that shakes the mirth
from dusty cobwebs
languishing
in the darkened corners
of forgotten dreams.

*If I can stir an emotion or help you identify something
that stirs your own memories, then I will have accomplished
something every writer dreams about.*

— *R. E. S.*

lost souls

Shadows ripple
while darkness climbs the steps of night.
Love weeps
awaiting an answer to the echoing ache
and the restless spirit
continues its endless journey alone.

diversity

Keep reaching out
until someone reaches back
to embrace tones of life
sensed by ringing sounds
of differences we share.
Listen for returning echoes
of sweeter understanding
as it begins to fill the hollow
in harmony with life
that the bell
and its tune completes.

Poetry helps us cope with the diversity of feelings, realities, and dreams of life. Stay in touch with your feelings, the magnificent world around you, and the people who fill your moments.

— R. E. S.

butterflies

I chased a butterfly
across a field.
It was beautiful.
Too colorful to keep
but willing to fly
while I lost my way
                    chasing it.

ephemeral

Love is a surrounding fog
touching everything
then slowly stealing away.

reason

My voice reaches out
as a beacon
spelling not words
but meanings.
Providing reason
dividing thought
a shining concept of confusion
emitted as a signal
for organization
to enter
and light the way
for shadows
and ideas
to find their place
within me.

twins

Two hands reach out
with hearts touching
as souls entwine forever
and love is the measured heartbeat
conquering time lonely
distance intolerable
and the cornered experience
examined by twins of emotion.

sunset

Between the pause of day and night
the sky excites itself
revealing plumage of soft pastel
as a bouquet of life's momentary color
reflected in the framed generosity of softness
the glare of fleeting legend
retires the busy day
fills the world of thought
with an introduction of
the approaching night child.

autumn

Autumn is wiping dew from the windshield
the warmth of an Indian summer day
brittle leaves that shuffle and break
the last green of a departing summer
children's merriment on the way to anywhere
Nature's way of saying thanks to the seasons
and all the brilliance of love.

mutual respect

Can we reside in
the echoing domain
of another person's dream?
Does the tone of challenge
immortalize the wish
before the flood of thought
becomes extinct?
Where do we blend truth
beyond garnished moments of hope?
We dare not stifle
the candidacy of understanding
or the chance to say
"I love you"
in the language of mutual respect.

rejections

Like a summer storm
blowing in, blowing out
she passed his gaze.
Bringing the wind in gusts
she swirled about his consciousness
demanding his full attention.
Her look darkened the closer she came.
He responded partly in fear
mostly in wonder.
He felt rather than saw lightning
as it brought a crackling intensity
to their imminent meeting.
Nothing he could do or say would alter
the course of this reunion
now lit by explosive electricity.
The smell of burnt sulfur
filled his nostrils
nearly suffocating his memory of her.
The confrontation was laden with broken promises
scattered dreams and a dust cloud of recollections
gliding past her innocence
running in front of her fury
looking for a home to bring this irrational meeting
to a summit of reality.
For years he had suspected she searched for him.
Now he was too tired to run
too strong to turn away
too conflicted to care if she found him
too sure of her intentions

to let this challenge go unanswered.
He opened his arms and heart
looked up in the moment of her approach and said
"I've always loved you, take me with you"
but she was gone before the words took form.
The moment she passed, his heart ached.
Wearing her rejection like rain
he fell to the ground
his dwindling emotions
mixed with tears, began to puddle
at the feet of his lost feelings.

memory

I walked the path around your eyes
and settled in your smile
to live, hidden
among the nearly forgotten treasures
of childhood toys
high school dances
first loves
Christmas seasons
and life's tearful disappointments.
Comforted by my place of rest
on the lighted side
of dust-gathering thoughts
threatened little by each new article
pushing me deeper
into the attic of memory
that will forever escape
the retiring brush
of a sweeping janitor's broom.

I hope these poems tap into your memory bank. Sometimes it is best to look between the lines, for there you might find the best memories and new insights. I'm grateful to have the chance to put these thoughts on the walls of your imagination.

— *R. E. S.*

pollyanna on display

I see your face in all I do.
I'm drawn to that look, now possessed.
Your eyes command my attention, too
just one look, my emotions obsessed.
Your perfect face, divided asunder
paralyzes all but irrational fear.
My heart beats as storm's loudest thunder
afraid if you called, I might not hear.
Your smile brightens each day of my life
your inviting lips do much the same.
I'd like to ask you to please be my wife
if only I had asked you, your name.

getting together

Love is
   a creaky old wooden bridge
   hopscotch course
   cement sidewalks
   or dusty winding paths
   leading to your door.

leaving it behind

The rope of indecision
can soon become
a noose of words
tied merely to condemn
the resisting compliance of action
in a race against ourselves.

adam's apple

The triumph of love
travels deep in man's wish
for self-expression.
It walks in other ways
on the axis of temptation
to touch with sounds
and fill moments
with decision crawling—
an apple bite lodged
deep in the throat of harmony.

reformation of desire

We sit in life's window
watching the puddles fill
of simple expression
to weep
when the audit of emotion subsides
knowing
the drink of happiness
is always sweeter than
the drink of alone
but not always as accessible.

key to success

Corridors beyond the doors
of absolute will be
revealed safely
in the existence of the evening
as we grow slow enough
to listen
in love
and strong enough
to turn beyond
each key of recollection.

leadership

If encouragement
   brings a friend closer
   to the face of understanding
   and drives fear
   to the curved position of remorse
if caring
   places happiness
   in the erect position
   of truthful pride
   within a body of knowledge
   that contains ego
   in the box of inner self
then you will have made leadership
   a congress of fact
   rather than
   an unheard petition of hope.

conjugal language

You can neither hurry
nor slow
the reservation of thought
or love.
Comfort remains
in the expression of silence
each brings to the other.

renaissance

Surrender my pen
the facility of words
to an artist's brush
so love
painted
in the captivating
color of memory
will rekindle
and stimulate
the inspiration of
together again.
The renaissance of desire.

satisfaction

The glare of life
that has passed
through the windows
of my years
is resolute
and comforting.

indian summer, love of all seasons

A cracked curled leaf
above the ground
freely floating
on its way down
once full of colors
now nondescript
unlike a kiss
from your sweet lips.

The pull of Indian summer takes me all the way back to Michigan and my boyhood—the hint of smoke before winter's blanket of snow.

— R. E. S.

especially for you

Be on the way to yourself
   your world will care that you do.
Songbirds sing of lessons learned
   always looking to serenade a new dawn.
Each day your song will reach someone
   who will touch others with that happiness.
The need for you will be even greater then
   and you will be responsible for immense love.

the optimist

Why is it when you see rain
I see rainbows?
When you see clouds
I see silver linings.
On the cusp of a brisk day
you fear winter is on its way.
I remain undaunted by your pessimism
but it is hard to discuss with you.
Instead of arguing about our differences
I'll continue to see the best in you
helping to stabilize our way.

from mother to daughter

As a lovely child
you wanted to look just like your mother
and life was good to both of you.
As a young lady
beauty filled you up and
she became more ordinary
causing a time of doubt
when you were afraid to mirror
what you had often thought about.
But love was steadfast
in each of you and
she was the teacher
who filled your personal vase
with long-stemmed lessons
mixed with special meanings deep within
a bouquet of caring, patience, love.
Laughter and sharing, when now put on display
remind me that you truly do
look just like your mother
and this verse tells it true.
I was there, saw it all, and testify
to having loved her, too.

robotic responses

Distance can be quantified
miles measured
space filled.

Time passes.
Energy burns.
Love dies.
Replacements ordered.

after the lights go out

When finally a mind is blinded
to activity's carillon pealing
as when the heart denies pleasure
of love's most precious feeling
with disposition no longer in question
dispelling fertile thought's thrill
the fresh air of life soon stales
as it most assuredly will.

Who then will argue the question
of how frightening tasks may have been?
Who will respond in discussion
of differences potential may lend
to the moment of forgiven indiscretion
which amplifies wrong from right
where belonging is memory awakened
and being is merely a light?

Will angels in the landscape blend
a pattern all may see?
Would there be room for "might have been"
had you not been here with me?
Aphonic songs reveal our choice
in chorus to the pattern
crescendoed voices through the land
as light escapes a lantern.

It's never better to be best
more often to be right. .
So in brilliance of the day
accept the dim of night.
And if you can't imagine angels
dancing through the wood
does it make you sad my friend?
Oh, don't you wish you could?

table of leftovers

The spell was cast
its bell was rung
light was bent
the dream begun.
Who slept upon
the midnight lace
of darkened night
that dreams once chased
across the rooms
of Christmas past
beyond the childhood
wishes stashed
to let the light
of daylight show
places where
my mind might go
if now examined with respect
holds more than conscious intellect.

a montage

I've seen the cape of sunset
wrapped around the dusk.
Watched the night sleep
in a bed of darkness
unaware
that dawn was dressing the day
in brilliance.
I've watched a smile leap
into the face of laughter
broken only
by the sounds of merriment.
I've witnessed this and more
knowing these things represent
the montage of your love.

contributions

The oracles of time
like rings on the trunk of a tree
designate Man
within the circumference
of his meager contributions
to the accomplishments
growing up around him.

*Creative spirits wish to leave something of themselves behind
for posterity. One song for the singer, one line for the actor, one
painting for the artist, and one poem from the poet.*

— R. E. S.

ad infinitum

Time touches the mountain
in a surrounding softness of cloud
as the spirit soars
to share the view
of times first thought
and loves first felt
as each stepped through
Heaven's open door.

classifications

In time
every part of the sea
touches the shore
as a wave, kissing
for the moment
sand and sea
taking, then leaving
some of each
to the environment
our togetherness creates.

We near our kiss
the wave full to crest.
Emotion lengthens the beach
along our shore.
We must wait
while life decides
whether we are rushing water
drying sand
or a single breath
in time.

The next poem is dedicated to my mother and father. I'm sorry she was not alive to read it, but I know she already knew the sentiments it expresses. The poem is one of my personal favorites.

— R. E. S.

indebtedness

You are the indelible mark
on the surface of my soul.
You poured the sand
upon the land
where I began to grow.
You showed me light
when there was night
provided shade from sun's harsh glow.
You provided love to form the face
of the man I've come to know.
Through fun and strife
you've shared my life
preparing me to be
good husband, father, and citizen
in the time and space of me.
Your sterling bits of wisdom spread
across my soul and in my head
to fill my heart and lifetime view
with all the things I learned from you.
Your examples were always
subtle and crisp
as I learned them along the way
lessons of life perfectly expressed
that I practice even today.
Time has moved the story's flow
you shaped my life in wisdom's glow.
It makes me glad, Mom and Dad
that you were there to know.

setting love free

She cut, but not to cause pain
thinning in guarded, tender weaning
to release the umbilical cord of love
setting free the child to grow
in memory knowing and being known.
The other end of the cord
would always be at home with her
so she set upon the world
as much of herself as loving would allow.

transition

Yesterday
      the drying sun
      shrunk a pond of memory
      replacing borrowed time
      with new experience.

Today
      the lusting breeze
      generates emotion through life
      within real time
      of unrelenting desire.

Tomorrow
      will be remaining hope
      when mountains of wind and water
      are brought together
      in generation's new-found choices.

what love is

Love is a dime in a penny roll
a smile on a gloomy day
rock gardens on an empty lot
lemonade stands of summer
the rising tide of an empty sea.
It's part of you and part of me.

Love is so many things, yet we each identify with it, and it makes us part of each other. I hope love invites you to continue exploring your own creativity.

— R. E. S.

74

support systems

Tomorrow started eons ago
taking forever to happen.
It seems like only yesterday
we wanted today to be over.
The business we look forward to
will have to wait again.
We must take time out for loving, living
and being each other's porch rail.

knowing who your friends are

Something smells
like piss and vinegar
burned eggs
scorched hair
like the dog wasn't let out in time.
Even in the open air
I'm beginning to know
exactly what you are
a lousy friend
no friend at all
a half-burned cheap cigar.

an engineering mentality

Getting to know some people
is like owning a ten-speed bike
and not being tall enough
to reach the pedals
or smart enough
to figure out the gears.

reaching potential

The knowledge of inner self
contrasts
purchased emotions of insecurity.
Truth
will always be heard
above the lecherous voices of mediocrity.
When people can grow
beyond the self-reflecting
purpose of their decision
accomplishments
will be nonrestrictive
and their goals
will be limitless.

*Few of us reach our own expectations. Fewer still maximize
our potential. We need to try harder. The benefits are
unbelievable.*

— R. E. S.

intruding moments

Sometimes we climb
the challenging mountain
only to find ourselves
swallowed by the view
that seems protected
by the pinnacle of exposure
diminished because we are there.
We are the journey.

northwest winds
and autumn leaves

Shaking branches to and fro
forceful winds upon the tree
until at last we are shown
unsettled moments, leaves are free.

Gracefully measured to descend
colored leaves drawn to the ground
dependent only upon time and space
until their winter home is found.

Blotting landscape's picturesque view
drifting buoyantly, freefall in flight
piled together by hands unseen
busy designing through day and night.

Colors diminished to dull brown
just before the winter snow
crunchy reminders under foot
of autumn brilliance we all know.

A full day of driving rain and howling wind inspired this poem. While the storm raged outside, my mind developed this calming image. This is the fun of writing. It can turn disaster into victory, love into tragedy, or capture color in a bouquet of words.

— R. E. S.

Christmas tree, oh Christmas tree

If I were
an enchanted tree
I'd grant three wishes
for people I'd see.
Of Nature's gifts
I would bestow
the dove of peace
would surely show.
Sheer impressions
of health for all
would likely be
my second call.
The third wish
festive as a sleigh
brings happiness now
and every day.
Rejoice in spirit of transition
on the road
to your ambition.

remembering nana

I first remember Nana
when I was maybe two.
Back then she let me have my way
"That's okay for you to do."
She'd hold me tightly in her arms
to say I was like Mom.
"She ruled the roost just like you, too,
with all her childish charm."
Nana let me stay with her
while Mama was away.
We'd spend hours playing
together. Every day
she'd brush my hair
then curl it, too, and
if I began to cry
"Don't worry, Sweetie, I'm here for you, and
that's okay for you to do."
So through the years her promise kept
she was always there for me.
Even as the years turned gray
her grandma's wise inflection
always ended thoughts to me
with self-assured direction.
She'd look me squarely in the eye
with a promise that was true
"If it makes you happy, go ahead;

that's okay for you to do."
As the years got in our way
her health took all but spunk away.
She lay upon the sheet so white
I knew she meant to die this night.
I held her hand to help her through
my tears fell hard upon my face.
She saw that I'd begun to cry
touched my cheek with this to say
"Don't worry, Sweetie, I'm here for you,
and that's okay for you to do."
I whispered, "Love you, Nana."
She said, "Love you, too."
I kissed her lips, she closed her eyes
a moment filled with last good-byes.

I was asked to write this poem to represent the spirit of my daughters' relationship with their maternal grandmother, after she passed away. It was difficult. She had great influence on my daughters. The poem seemed to take forever to write. I cried after every couple of lines. I hope it truly captures the spirit of her life entwined with my daughters' lives.

— R. E. S.

the mountain's highest peak

Love upon a mountain of fire
our naked souls to share
wind across our tender skin
sensation's warming flare.
Insistent autumn winds soon blow
nagging doubt away
assuage forever feelings of fear
embedded in our turgid play.
Freedom of this moment's pleasure
lasting now in memories bright
lingering tendrils of passion's measure
the fading penumbra of the night.

good-bye ice and snow

Winter rain
writing silken letters
on the floor of my
forgotten yesterday
glares glistening
wistfully at my
saddened memory
while sunshine
touching my face
erases last doubts
of decisions past.
Time is the closet
where we store
most of our lives.
Mountainous dreams
hung on crossbars
of winter sleep, now melting
to rest in desert's dawn
where flowers grow
from spring's first breath
to hide the dying snow.

where we all live

Reason and order
kept in delicate balance
cause one to feel discombobulated
by unreasonableness or disorderliness.
We cannot keep up with
what is slowly delivered on muscled legs
and
deliberate strides of social change.
Impacts happen before we are aware and
become integrated into our consciousness
before change is mirrored
on the backs of public behavior.

elements of a relationship

You are an angry part of me
in a tangled war of words.
The trauma of our dissension
has had no time to heal.
From a garden of hope
can we pick flowers of conciliation?
Even the sun decides some gentle things
in shadows.

lilacs

I once picked a flower
a lilac of sound
its color and fragrance, my will to abound
acquiring my senses, even today
as a flower and friend newly found.

But in life there are lilies and
daisies in motion
a bouquet of others to see
applied like a lotion
on the variety of choices
for each experience and emotion to be.

I still favor lilacs
and for all good reasons
yet a June rose came into my life.
I appreciate lilies, especially in verse
and daisies and mums in a pride.
But the June rose will last
as the flower of my seasons
especially the one that's my wife.

rain and memories

Rain comes and goes
except in the meantime it is a part of
flowers and grass.
Wind wails and blows
except in the meantime it is what
holds the kite up.
The scent of summer
runs in front of the storm
belonging to rain, wind, and me.

a wind of hope

Our love rests in the hurricane's eye
Calm now
but the heaviest winds
are on the way.
Survival depends
on how well we can bend
with the wind.

nightmares

I'd like to say goodnight now
but silence ignores me
and loneliness screams at me
to be still.

impressions

I'm impressed by the vastness of the sea
all it takes
and what it gives.
The beauty of the mountains awes me.
How nearly close
yet distant they are.
I am awake with life within a dream
yet I sleep in; thoughts of where you are
and what you've done
to make me conscious of what I've seen.

law of love

The law of love
like the language
is universal in meaning
vague in definition
and common in practice.

quiet

Sometimes
the silence of what we say
is better than
the lonely vigil we observe
in preparation for
the echoing indulgence
of self-deceit.

lover's prayer

Let us kiss the bright tomorrow
with our understanding of today.
Together let us hold the unknown
as we share the trusting hope
of more than we presently are.
We can thank the world for turning
slowly enough for us to be each other
yet fast enough to turn us into one.

This poem was one of the first written during my stay in Palm Springs. On this particular day, I became enthralled with the beautiful sunrise.

— R. E. S.

eye opener

The sun in the morning
is often a warning
that suddenly we must face
the rest of the day.

delicately beaten

I have been bruised
by the strength of earth
men's hands
and noise.
Words have practiced cunning upon me
but will that I survive
the extraction of soul
by the softest thing I've known.
The delicacy of love lost.

*I imagine these thoughts will move anyone who has loved
and lost. In this case, I know it was better to have loved than not
to have loved at all.*

—R. E. S.

dancing with shadows

Shadows danced along the wall
yet never left the floor.
While in the light
they quickly moved
in and out of every door, and
as they grew
then shrank from view
they never seemed to fall
just jump and jerk
their ghostly dance
performed before us all.

the best of friends

I miss you dear friend.
Where are you that I can't
find you in everything I do?
Though miles part us
or separated by time
we are standing together in
every memory.
We shall revive our friendship
when next we meet
as though paralleled in
everything we do.
Nothing can come between us.
Our lives are forever changed
by knowing the truest meaning
of friendship.
Our past lives and present existence
become entwined as we plan the
uncertain future together.

you are special

Special friends are hard to find
but what makes you rarer still
is that you treat
the friends you've found
as families often will.

A reader can usually guess what the writer's mood suggests.
While some readers are lost in a poem or line, others find hidden
treasures of delight. We can find ourselves in their substance.
At times, we swear the author read our mind and captured our
heart and life. I hope you have found at least one poem that calls
to you and becomes your own.

— *R. E. S.*

what you are to me

You are more than the way you look
it is how you see things.
You are more than the way you walk
it is the direction you choose.
It is not how often you love
but rather how much love you share.
It is not that you profess to love me
but that you demonstrate love's fullest
meaning.

just friends

When I need someone to talk to
you are there to listen.
When I need a helping hand
I feel comforted that yours is there.
When I need a smile
to light my way
show compassion
or hold the world at bay
yours is first to heal depression
change my mood
or brighten the day.
I'm indebted to you for
the willingness you show
to bring stability into my life.
All that you give
I hope to repay in kind
for friendship upon which I depend.
When my contract comes due
I hope to emulate you as a true
rather than marginal friend.

Puyallup
seems so far away
from rain that falls on
Redmond

Ink, not dry on the most recent pages of life
chapters rushing to conclusion
others folding, tearing, deliberately crushing
the paper, by their own interpretation.
Changes occurring belong to the future
and they are mine to decide
as it relates to me.
Storybooks are written one page at a time
but that depends on how long
the cloud bank stays open for business.
Isn't it amazing how a smile
can brighten either place
and cause even rain to reflect
the happiness one now brings the other?

the oar of integrity

Awash in a sea of Pity Me
the raft that takes us there
is compromised ability
to wit I won't prepare.
It's politics that spreads the sea
before the bow aloof
then ripples through the rest of me
to miss the mark of truth.
We entrust responsibility
to chart a course begun
while at the helm authority
corrupts the needs be done.
Selfish eyes in fixed gaze stare
upon this foolish quest.
Never a glimpse at might be fair
devoid of what is best.
Deep within this tragedy
from which I am apart
the trauma of the travesty
denies what's in my heart.
A loathsome crew controls the show
of this raft whose journey bound
will only see the turbulence below
their logic starved or drowned.

Destiny can never bend
or yield without a voice.
To ask aloud, where will it end?
and exercise—a choice.
So steer again without discourse
their rudder soiled and tainted.
Now raise the oar integrity
your strength in truth resolved
direct these fools from immorality
away from fear dissolved.

making the right decisions

"And what if...?" is always tendered by
  the mercies of indecision.
"And why not...?" is usually accompanied by
  the bullish currier of impatience.
"Perhaps" or "Maybe" are wrapped
  in harmonious cloaks of confidence
  yet to descend upon the question.
"Yes" is an affirmation
  which propagates new questions.

knowing you — knowing me

I find the expression of you
in the bouquet of love you bring
to our relationship.
Each flower reveals a different mood.
Every petal suggests new hope.
Each color radiates separate desires.
All, united in your fragrance.
Even in your absence
the bouquet fills the room
keeping each moment alive
freshening the next
bringing my senses to attention
within the pleasure of
my imagination.

the eulogy

There is a time in our lives
when all that is left
is to spend our final goodbye.
Love is deathless
living beyond us
though we die.
As I bring these words together
I am still between
the former and the latter
laboring to accept the burden
of providing you relief
from the universe of your sorrow
that which you must endure
when I am at last, no longer.
Be certain as I approach the unknown
I fear no fear, but would shed a tear
if I thought you might somehow forget me.
There is relief in action.
Stay busy feeding our memories.
Whatever else I have given up in my lifetime
none is greater treasure than my family
none more beautiful a jewel than your friendship
or as radiant as love we have shared.

To all of you, please accept
as part of my legacy
as part of my gift to you
my heartfelt, love-sent good-bye.
Know with surety the last sound I heard
was that of the wind
as it wandered empty corridors
of my memory's final design.
All that remains is yours to write
pages of my life, embraced by my death
signed in your own hand
so I can live on within you.

déjà vu

Something about what you were and are
lives within the shadow of every thought
sharing mood and movement.
Your brilliance lights my day
while your softness settles around me
like the night, to stay awhile
holding me like a familiar comforter
on a warm bed
bringing me back, wanting.

goodnight

Sun falls gently
between the wind and water
of a crooked smile
so full of love
it cannot help
but somehow
be affected by it
like a shadow
passing dark in the night.

the uncertainty of life

Which is stronger?
To like or to love?
Are they each a part of the other
if they are at all?
Or do they live a separate way
defined by a war of feelings
that protests the past
before the moment of reality
joins the uncertain generosity
of a new day?

*My father passed away at the age of eighty-nine. A poet
himself, he encouraged my outlook on "love in the past, the
present, and the future." His support of me, and confidence in
me, stimulated my efforts. I miss him. I hope his influence will
always show up in my work. He helped me reach beyond my safe
zone to find the words so you and I could connect.*

— R. E. S.

quiet please

The quiet of thought
is different than
the quiet of alone.
It can be shared
later
when the need to be quiet
is greater than
the need to be alone.

a cloak for my love

If I am only fog
shrouding the dark of night
save me no malice
in your love or reputation.
Understanding will be your comfort.
Missing you will be my remorse.
My burden, the cross of my decision
never to apologize for loving you.

portrait of perfection

Paint dries slowly on life's canvas
as a blurred vision
to live in dominance of
the surrounding motion
as vibrancy
created by love
emanates from
the purpose you have given
to the distracting face of tomorrow.

the air we breathe

May the breath of love
express itself
on our relationship
as another beautiful day
so others will be affected
by all we share.

as big as Texas

Darkness in a nighttime mood
the sun had run alone.
Quiet yawned above desire
and the dimension of it all
is where love once stood.

In the beginning, I wrote, collected, stored, revived, revised, collected again, and finally published so others could enjoy what had been gathering in my memory bank over the years.

For a long while, my fear was that perhaps I would break the bank, run out of things to share, and then I would have to go home and play with my mental blocks. But much to my surprise, the thoughts keep coming and through it all, I am still evolving along with the poetry I write.

— R. E. S.

the missing link

A noiseless quiet transcends
the desert heat.
Desperate thoughts of love prevail.
Empty arms and full desire
my need and loneliness
travel alone to meet you.
The journey ends
where it began
in the streets of your first smile
in our hello
in love's beginning.

astronomically challenged

Traveling through
the daylight of my life
I wonder aloud
"What have I now?"
Approaching the black abyss
of unknown night
I wonder to myself
"What will be then?"
As the hours are lit
without the sun
as the moon appears
from west to east
I chase the dreams
across the sky
living in doubt
wondering
"Why?"

opposites attract

The lines to show
where our paths have crossed
are very plainly there.
The trouble is that you're a circle
and I am still a square.
The moment that our lives were touched
was very clearly drawn.
The trouble is that I am dusk
and surely you are dawn.
So come and kiss the rain away
and make the darkness bright.
Together we can share the world
where you'll be day
and I will be the night.

family trees

I looked at trees
  and they were inviting.
I talked to them
  and they listened well.
I admired their strengths
  and compared them to humans.

Trees won.

grandpa

I miss the comforting smile
worn by the man we called Grandpa.
When he smiled
everything was right with the world.
I miss his hands
mixing cookie dough into Spicy Devil's Food Delights
causing my mouth to weep with weakness
for just one more bite.
I miss the heart
beating regularly for those he loved
enriching the lives of people he'd meet
strangers who would share
the mantle of his kindness.
I miss the Sloppy Joes or soup he'd blend
to share with family and friends
hoping to relieve the coldest part of their day
from hunger, emotional stress, or life's many
trials and tribulations.
I miss watching him delight children
taking them on adventures through stories
teaching them tricks of tying their shoes or
how to catch the first fish ever
lessons of patience we all must learn.
Gone, too, is his wise counsel
often given in choices we needed to make
served, like his cookies, to be devoured
one idea at a time, filled with the ingredients
of hope, strength, and love
so we'd find solution to our issues.

I miss this man who so loved his role as Grandpa
knowing he can never be replaced in our
world of differing perspectives
feeling worn down by the loss shared by so many.
He will be remembered each time I look into a mirror
where he can be found in my own face, graying hair
and wrinkled skin.
Others will see him, too, in what I do
to emulate the richness he shared with all of us.
He will be remembered each time someone
calls me Grandpa, too.

love lost in the space of me

I'm searching for
missing parts
forgotten thoughts
broken dreams
weeping hearts
those we know
those who care
to help me mourn
a love still there.

rainbows are more than water and sun

Rainbows are the bridge between friends
the path between realities.
They are the reminder that we are infinitely
less important than Nature, God
or our opinion of ourselves.
Rainbows are the primary colors
the pastels we see in all we remember.
They are reminders that everything in life
comes and goes even while we are watching
unaware of the change until it is gone.

comatose

I thought I'd tell you
how much I love you
but what I think or say
apparently doesn't make up
the difference between living and dying.
I don't want our lives
spent in parallel ages or worlds
so please wake up and listen
while I tell you I'm sorry and
I miss you more every day.

retirement looming

No place to go and
no hurry to get there.
Undaunted, I move in the direction
of habit's selected path
pulled along by what is envisioned as the
release from the past, rushing toward
new experiences.
Contributing to my legacy is identity's shadow
what I've become tripping on the hope
of defining what I'd rather be.
Time interjects the need to hurry
before opportunity to design my journey
closes doors to future choices.

flying in our own shadow

When we peel back the cowling of our lives
to examine that which propels us forward
we can almost see our old self
standing in the shadow of
where we'd like to be.
With each look, the vision changes
as do we with each success or failure
on the way to our unknown destiny.

waiting is only perspective

Waiting is spending useless time
in useful ways
convincing yourself the reason for the wait
is worth the inconvenience of being there.

Observation makes the wait more enjoyable.
Mind games manipulate "what ifs"
and "what might have beens"
helping sort reality from memory
truth from fiction
meeting new in pools of reflections past.

Waiting fills in the crossword puzzle
of life's more tedious moments
regardless of how long it takes
to satisfy your need to be there.
Waiting...just waiting.

a Key West experience

Palm fronds blowing
in weathered wind
disturbing shadows
cast in shade.
The sun falls hot
on blistering skin
turning pleasure
into a charade
spoiling an appreciation
of this picturesque view
from the palm tree's beauty
to loving thoughts of you.

Key West sunset

Standing in a golden hue
of sun surrendering to a rest
wrapped in magical colors
quiet moments of emerging quest.
Chase away the bright of day.
Bring shadows to the night.
Dramatic overture on display
slips quietly by, then out of sight
disappearing beyond the western shelf.
We watch the once-bright moment's glare
our hearts stop briefly to skip a beat
and capture memories, now to share.

*With the sun now setting, it is time to call a halt. I hope you
have enjoyed our journey together. I invite you to share again
with me soon.*

— R. E. S.

Poems alphabetically by title

134

Poems by theme

137

140